Learn to Read
Ukrainian in 5 Days

ALEX KOVALENKO

ISBN: 978-1519561923

CONTENTS

Introduction   i

Unit 1 – а, е, о, к, м, т   1

Unit 2 – і, р, с, в   3

Unit 3 – у, н, х, б   7

Unit 4 – л, п, д, з   9

Unit 5 – и, ч, ц, ж   11

Unit 6 – й, г, ш, щ   13

Unit 7 – я, ї, ю, є   15

Unit 8 – г, ф   17

Unit 9 – ь, '   19

Unit 10 – Doubled Consonants   21

Unit 11 – Review   23

Ukrainian Alphabet   25

Glossary – Thematic Order   27

Glossary – Alphabetical Order   35

INTRODUCTION

Learning a new alphabet can be very intimidating for an English speaker only used to reading the Latin alphabet. This is partly why English speakers tend to stick to learning other languages that use the same alphabet, such as French, Spanish and Italian – because they seem a lot easier!

But learning a new alphabet does not have to be so difficult. The difficulty is finding a good system to learn the new alphabet so that you don't get discouraged and give up before you make real progress. Making progress in the language is the best motivator.

The secret to learning a new alphabet is to be taught how to pronounce each letter separately, and then to practice how the new letters combine with letters you already know to read real words in the alphabet in a structured way. This is not revolutionary – it is most likely how you learned to read English – but it is not easy to find for other languages.

This book will teach you how to read the Ukrainian alphabet in exactly that way, and with this method you will be able to read Ukrainian in only 5 days or less! After that you will be able to enjoy the Ukrainian language and culture in a way that you were never able to before.

THE UKRAINIAN ALPHABET
українська абетка

The Ukrainian language uses 33 letters of the Cyrillic alphabet and is written from left to right. It uses the same basic letters as some other Slavic languages, such as Russian and Bulgarian, as well as several non-Slavic languages from the former U.S.S.R. Although Ukrainian uses the same alphabet as Russian, there are differences in pronunciation between some of the letters in Ukrainian and

Russian, just as there are differences in pronunciation between French, Spanish and English even though they use the same alphabet.

Although it is different from the Latin alphabet used to write English (and other European languages) the Ukrainian alphabet is not a difficult alphabet to learn to read. This is because, with almost no exceptions, letters are pronounced as they are written and written as they are pronounced in Ukrainian, unlike languages like English that make use of a lot of silent letters and historical spellings.

Like the Latin alphabet used to write English, the Ukrainian alphabet has both upper and lowercase letters. Upper case letters are used at the beginning of a sentence and in proper nouns. In Ukrainian most of the uppercase letters are the same shape as the lowercase letters - they are just bigger.

HOW TO USE THIS COURSE

The primary goal of this course book is to teach the reader to recognize the Ukrainian alphabet and to begin to read the Ukrainian language.

The main way this is accomplished is by teaching the individual pronunciations of each letter, and then utilizing "Practice" sections where the reader can practice reading real Ukrainian words. These "Practice" sections are very important and the main way the reader will start to feel comfortable with the Ukrainian alphabet. The answers to all "Practice" questions are included directly below the questions, but try to avoid looking at the answers until you have attempted to answer the questions yourself.

Throughout the book, the reader will also learn approximately 150 real Ukrainian words. These words have been carefully selected to be of maximum benefit to beginner students of the language and are a great starting point for students who want to continue their study of Ukrainian. In the end of the book there are two glossaries

– one in thematic order and one in alphabetical order – where the student can study and memorize all the words learned in this course.

The course material has been designed to be completed slowly over 5 days, while reviewing lessons as necessary. You are encouraged to go at whatever pace you feel comfortable with and to feel free to go back to lessons to review as much as needed.

Good luck and I hope you enjoy the first step on your journey to learning the Ukrainian language.

UNIT 1 - а, е, о, к, м, т

The first 6 letters introduced in this course are the letters in Ukrainian that resemble English letters and are pronounced roughly the same. Basically you already know these six Ukrainian letters!

The letter а in Ukrainian is pronounced like the "a" sound in the English words "spa" or "father" (IPA: /ɑ/). Remember to pronounce this word like a long "a" and not a short "a" sound like in the English words "cat" or "apple". The uppercase form is A.

The letter е is pronounced like the "e" sound in the English words "met" or "peg" (IPA: /ɛ/). The uppercase form is E.

The letter о is pronounced like the "o" sound in the English word "not" or "octopus" (IPA: /ɔ/). The uppercase form is O.

The letter к is pronounced like the "k" sound in the English words "kick" or "kite" (IPA: /k/). The uppercase form is K.

The letter м is pronounced like the "m" sound in the English words "mother" or "Michael" (IPA: /m/). The uppercase form is M.

The letter т is pronounced like the "t" sound in the English words "tan" or "Tom" (IPA: /t/). The uppercase form is T.

As you can see these 6 letters are virtually the same as in English!

PRACTICE

Try to recognize these English words in their Ukrainian disguises.
The answers are below.

1. ат
2. мет
3. кат
4. так
5. кот
6. мат
7. мама

ANSWERS

1. at
2. met
3. cat
4. tack
5. cot
6. mat
7. mama

UNIT 2 - i, p, c, в

The four letters introduced in this unit look like letters you already know, but unlike Unit 1 these letters are not pronounced the same as in English. Pay close attention to these letters and avoid pronouncing them like in English.

The letter i is pronounced like the "ee" in "tree", or the "i" in "spaghetti" (IPA: /i/). It is not pronounced like the "i" in "pit" or the "i" in "spite". It will be represented by "i" in this book. The uppercase form is I.

The letter p is pronounced like the Spanish "r" sound in "rapido", i.e. a trilled or rolled "r" sound (IPA: /r/). This letter is not difficult to pronounce for an English speaker but does require some practice. If you cannot pronounce this letter yet, you can substitute an English "r" sound for now. Although this letter resembles an English "p" it is not pronounced like a "p" sound. The uppercase form is P.

The letter c is pronounced like the "s" sound in "some" or "same" (IPA: /s/). Although it resembles an English "c", it is never pronounced like the "c" in "cat". It is always pronounced with an "s" sound. The hard "c" sound is spelled with к in Ukrainian. The uppercase form is C.

The letter в is pronounced like the "v" sound in "very" (IPA: /v/). Sometimes you will hear a "w" sound instead of a "v" sound, but the beginner student should think of this letter as a "v" sound. Although it resembles an uppercase "B", it is never pronounced like the English "b" sound in "boy". The uppercase form is B.

PRACTICE 1

Try to recognize these English words in their Ukrainian disguises. Focus on the correct pronunciation and not necessarily the English spelling. The answers are below.

1. рат
2. ті
3. сіт
4. вет
5. матс
6. котс
7. рот
8. тім
9. стем
10. сторм

ANSWERS 1

1. rat
2. tea
3. seat
4. vet
5. mats
6. cots
7. rot
8. team
9. stem
10. storm

PRACTICE 2

Try to read these real Ukrainian words. The English translation is given next to each word. The correct pronunciations are given in the answers below.

1. кава   (coffee)
2. море   (sea)
3. ріка   (river)
4. сім   (seven)
5. вісім   (eight)

ANSWERS 2

1. kava
2. more
3. rika
4. sim
5. visim

UNIT 3 - y, н, x, б

The Ukrainian letter y is pronounced like the "oo" sound in "boot" or the end of the word "shoe" (IPA: /u/). Although this letter resembles an English "y", it is not pronounced like the "y" sound in "yesterday" or the "y" sound in "tiny". This letter will be represented as "u" in this book. The uppercase form is У.

The Ukrainian letter н is pronounced like the "n" sound in "now" or "hen" (IPA: /n/). Pay close attention to this letter as it resembles an uppercase "H" in English, but should not be pronounced like an "h" sound. The uppercase form is Н.

The pronunciation of the Ukrainian letter x does not exist in English. It is the "ch" sound in the German "doch" or the "j" sound in the Spanish "ojos" (IPA: /x/). It is a heavy throat clearing "h" sound, or as a student once told me "a sound like choking on a chicken bone!" This letter will be represented by "kh" in this book. The uppercase form is X.

The letter б is pronounced like the "b" sound in "best" (IPA: /b/). Pay close attention to the letters б and в. The letter б, which looks like the number "6", is pronounced "b" and the letter в, which looks like an uppercase "B", is pronounced "v". With some practice this will become easier. The uppercase form is Б.

THE ACCENT IN UKRAINIAN

In Ukrainian, like in English, to pronounce a word correctly one must stress one syllable more than the rest. Also like English, the accent in Ukrainian is not normally written. Think about the English word conduct. It can be pronounced CONduct, or conDUCT although the written language does not tell us which

7

one is correct. This is the same as the situation in Ukrainian.

In Ukrainian-English dictionaries you will often see an accent written on the vowel that is to be stressed in the Ukrainian word. These accents, however, are not normally written in the language and therefore I will not be including them in the Ukrainian words in this book. However, I have included the accent in the pronunciation so that readers can start thinking in terms of the correct pronunciation and not develop bad habits of pronunciation that will have to be unlearned later.

PRACTICE

Try to read these real Ukrainian words. The English translation is given next to each word. The correct pronunciations (with accents) are given in the answers below.

1. вухо	(ear)
2. рука	(hand/arm)
3. ніс	(nose)
4. ні	(no)
5. небо	(sky)
6. особа	(person)
7. брат	(brother)
8. субота	(Saturday)

ANSWERS

1. vúkho
2. rukhá
3. nis
4. ni
5. nébo
6. osóba
7. brat
8. subóta

UNIT 4 - л, п, д, з

The Ukrainian letter л is pronounced like the "l" sound in "little" or "like" (IPA: /l/). The uppercase form is Л.

The letter п is pronounced like the "p" sound in "pie" or "pepper" (IPA: /p/). The Ukrainian letter resembles the Greek letter pi that you probably remember from geometry. This is not a coincidence as the Cyrillic alphabet derives from the Greek alphabet and some letters are close to the same. The uppercase form is П.

The letter д is pronounced like the "d" sound in "dad" (IPA: /d/). The uppercase form is Д.

The letter з is pronounced like the "z" in "zoo" or "zebra" (IPA: /z/). The uppercase form is З.

PRACTICE

Try to read these Ukrainian words. The English translation is given next to each word. The correct pronunciations are given in the answers below.

1. літак   (airplane)
2. стіл   (table)
3. тіло   (body)
4. хліб   (bread)
5. птах   (bird)
6. аеропорт   (airport)
7. двері   (door)
8. борода   (beard)

9. лід   (ice)
10. завтра   (tomorrow)
11. озеро   (lake)
12. понеділок   (Monday)

ANSWERS

1. liták
2. stil
3. tílo
4. khlib
5. ptakh
6. aeropórt
7. dvéri
8. borodá
9. lid
10. závtra
11. ózero
12. ponedílok

UNIT 5 - и, ч, ц, ж

The Ukrainian letter **и**, which looks like an uppercase "N" written backwards, is pronounced like the "i" sound in "pit" (IPA: /ɪ/). Note that this is not the same sound as the Ukrainian letter i. To distinguish these two letters, **и** will be represented in this book as "y" as this is standard practice when writing Ukrainian words in English. Remember however that this is a short "i" sound and not a "y" sound or an "ee" sound. The uppercase form is **И**.

The letter **ч** is pronounced like the "ch" sound in "church" (IPA: /tʃ/). Although written with two letters in English, it is really a single sound and is only written with one letter in Ukrainian. This letter will be represented in this book by č. The uppercase form is **Ч**.

The letter **ц** is pronounced like the "ts" sound in "cats" (IPA: /ts/). This is really two sounds, a "t" sound followed by an "s" sound, but it is written with only one letter in Ukrainian. When writing Ukrainian words in English this letter is often represented by a "c", but in this book I will use "ts" to avoid confusion with the English "c" sound. Unlike English, in Ukrainian this letter can be used at the beginning of a word and is still pronounced "ts". The uppercase form is **Ц**.

The letter **ж** is pronounced like the "s" sound in "pleasure" or "measure" (IPA: /ʒ/). This letter will be represented in this book as ž. The uppercase form is **Ж**.

PRACTICE

Try to read these Ukrainian words. The English translation is given next to each word. The correct pronunciations are given in the answers below.

1. риба	(fish)
2. син	(son)
3. ринок	(market)
4. сорочка	(shirt)
5. чотири	(four)
6. сонце	(sun)
7. серце	(heart)
8. жінка	(woman)
9. книжка	(book)
10. університет	(university)

ANSWERS

1. rýba
2. syn
3. rýnok
4. soróčka
5. čotýry
6. sóntse
7. sértse
8. žínka
9. knýžka
10. universytét

UNIT 6 - й, г, ш, щ

The letter **й** is pronounced like the "y" sound in "toy", i.e. it creates a rising diphthong out of the preceding vowel (IPA: /j/). The letter **й** consists of the letter **и** with a breve above it, but it is a separate letter in Ukrainian. It will be represented as either an "i" or a "y" in this book after another vowel to attempt to represent the pronunciation without causing confusion. The uppercase form is **Й**.

The letter **г** is pronounced approximately like the English "h" sound in "behind". You will hear some speakers pronounce this letter with a more "breathy" puff of air, or even as a more guttural sound (IPA: /ɦ/). For the purposes of reading Ukrainian, a beginner can consider this letter a simple "h" sound; however one should be aware that native speakers may pronounce it differently. This letter should always be pronounced in Ukrainian, even if it at the end of a syllable or word. The uppercase form is **Г**.

The letter **ш** is pronounced like the "sh" sound in "short" (IPA: /ʃ/). Although written with two letters in English, it is really one sound and it is written with one letter in Ukrainian. This letter will be represented in this book by š. The uppercase form is **Ш**.

The letter **щ** is pronounced like the "shch" sound in "fresh cheese" (IPA: /ʃtʃ/). This letter represents a sound that is a "sh" followed by a "ch", a **ш** followed by a **ч**. These two sounds are written with one letter in Ukrainian. It will be represented by "šč" in this book. The uppercase form is **Щ**.

PRACTICE

Try to read these Ukrainian words. The English translation is given next to each word. The correct pronunciations are given in the answers below.

1. чай   (tea)
2. червоний   (red)
3. чорний   (black)
4. друг   (friend)
5. голова   (head)
6. нога   (foot/leg)
7. шапка   (hat)
8. школа   (school)
9. кішка   (cat)
10. дощ   (rain)
11. сніг   (snow)
12. гора   (mountain)

ANSWERS

1. čai
2. červónyy
3. čórnyy
4. druh
5. holová
6. nohá
7. šápka
8. škóla
9. kíška
10. došč
11. snih
12. horá

UNIT 7 - я, ї, ю, є

The four letters introduced in this unit all begin with a "y" sound followed by a vowel sound.

The letter я is pronounced like the "ya" sound in "yard" (IPA: /jɑ/). This letter looks like a backwards capital "R". The uppercase form is Я.

The letter ї is pronounced with a "y" sound followed by i (IPA: /ji/). The uppercase form is Ї. Notice that the uppercase form still has the two dots above the letter.

The letter ю is pronounced like the "yu" sound in "yule" (IPA: /ju/). The uppercase form is Ю.

The letter є is pronounced like the "ye" sound in "yes" (IPA: /jɛ/). The uppercase form is Є.

PRACTICE

Try to read these Ukrainian words. The English translation is given next to each word. The correct pronunciations are given in the answers below.

1. неділя   (Sunday)
2. яблуко   (apple)
3. їжа   (food)
4. Україна   (Ukraine)
5. лютий   (February)
6. брюки   (pants)

7. Я є	(I am)
8. одяг	(clothing)
9. лікарня	(hospital)
10. країна	(country)

ANSWERS

1. nedílya
2. yábluko
3. yíža
4. ukrayína
5. lyútyy
6. bryúky
7. ya ye
8. ódyah
9. likárnya
10. krayína

UNIT 8 - ґ, ф

The letter ґ looks like the letter г but with an upturn. It is pronounced like the "g" sound in "good" or "goose" (IPA: /g/). This sound is not present in native Ukrainian words, but is used mostly for foreign borrowings. The uppercase form is Ґ.

The letter ф is pronounced like the "f" sound in "far" (IPA: /f/). This letter is also present in few native Ukrainian words and is mostly used in foreign borrowings. The uppercase form is Ф.

PRACTICE

Try to recognize these Ukrainian words that have been borrowed from English. Try to guess the pronunciation and the English word. The answers are below.
1. Ґуґл
2. Фейсбук

ANSWERS

1. Google
2. Facebook

UNIT 9 - ь, '

The letter **ь** is called a soft sign. The soft sign is normally written after a consonant and indicates its "softening" (technically called palatalization). What this means is that a soft "y" sound is added to the normal consonant sound causing it to sound "soft". I will show this letter in the pronunciation with a **ь** since it is difficult to show in English, but should not be ignored. Speaking correct Ukrainian involves "softening" the consonants when required.

The apostrophe ' is not really a letter in Ukrainian, but it is used a lot in the spelling of words. Technically, ' is the opposite of **ь**, meaning that it takes a "soft" consonant and makes it "hard" again. It is used before the vowels **я, ï, ю**, and **є**, i.e. the vowels with a "y" sound, to indicate that the preceding consonant should be given its full sound. Beginning students can basically ignore the apostrophe when it comes to pronunciation, and consider it just part of spelling correctly - the difference is very subtle and difficult to differentiate for beginners.

PRACTICE

Try to read these Ukrainian words. Pay attention to the **ь** and the '. The English translation is given next to each word. The correct pronunciations are given in the answers below.

1. кінь   (horse)
2. автомобіль   (car)
3. м'ясо   (meat)
4. п'ять   (five)
5. січень   (March)
6. квітень   (April)
7. дев'ять   (nine)
8. п'ятниця   (Friday)

ANSWERS

1. kinь
2. avtomobílь
3. m'yáso
4. p'yatь
5. síčenь
6. kvítenь
7. dév'yatь
8. p'yátnytsya

UNIT 10 - DOUBLED CONSONANTS

In Ukrainian, when consonants are written doubled, they are held for longer than if they were only written as a single consonant. In linguistics this feature is called gemination.

English does not do this within a word. The pronunciation of the first and second "g" sound in "baggage" are the same even though the first one is doubled.

English does have this feature between word boundaries however. Think of the difference between "night rain" and "night train". The "t" sound in the second example is held longer.

In Ukrainian, gemination does exist within a word. Just remember to hold the pronunciation a little longer when the consonant is written doubled, like in the "night train" example above. This will be shown in the pronunciation by doubling the consonant.

PRACTICE

Try to read these Ukrainian words. The English translation is given next to each word. The correct pronunciations are given in the answers below.

1. плаття   (dress)
2. обличчя   (face)
3. волосся   (hair)

ANSWERS

1. pláttya
2. oblýččya
3. volóssya

UNIT 11 - REVIEW

PRACTICE 1

Review the previous lessons by reading these real Ukrainian place names below. The correct pronunciations are given in the answers below.

1. Україна
2. Київ
3. Одеса
4. Харків
5. Львів
6. Дніпро
7. Крим
8. Синевир

ANSWERS 1

1. Ukrayína
2. Kýyiv (Kiev)
3. Odésa
4. Khárkiv
5. Lьviv
6. Dnipó (Dnieper)
7. Krim (Crimea)
8. Synevýr

PRACTICE 2

Review what you have learned in this book by reading the Ukrainian names below. The correct pronunciations are given in the answers below.

1. Порошенко
2. Янукович
3. Ющенко
4. Яценюк
5. Тимошенко
6. Кличко
7. Мельник
8. Коваленко

ANSWERS 2

1. Porošénko
2. Yanukóvič
3. Yúščenko
4. Yatsenyúk
5. Tymošénko
6. Klyčkó
7. Mélьnyk
8. Kovalénko

UKRAINIAN ALPHABET

Uppercase	Lowercase	Pronunciation
А	а	[a]
Б	б	[b]
В	в	[v]
Г	г	[h]
Ґ	ґ	[g]
Д	д	[d]
Е	е	[e]
Є	є	[ye]
Ж	ж	[ž]
З	з	[z]
И	и	[y]
І	і	[i]
Ї	ї	[yi]
Й	й	[i/y]
К	к	[k]

Л	л	[l]
М	м	[m]
Н	н	[n]
О	о	[o]
П	п	[p]
Р	р	[r]
С	с	[s]
Т	т	[t]
У	у	[u]
Ф	ф	[f]
Х	х	[kh]
Ц	ц	[ts]
Ч	ч	[č]
Ш	ш	[š]
Щ	щ	[šč]
Ь	ь	[ь]
Ю	ю	[yu]
Я	я	[ya]

GLOSSARY – THEMATIC ORDER

ANIMALS

тварина	[tvarýna]	animal
собака	[sobáka]	dog
кішка	[kíška]	cat
риба	[rýba]	fish
птах	[ptakh]	bird
корова	[koróva]	cow
свиня	[svynyá]	pig
миша	[mýša]	mouse
кінь	[kinь]	horse

PEOPLE

особа	[osóba]	person
мати	[máty]	mother
мама	[máma]	mommy / mama
батько	[bátьko]	father
тато	[táto]	daddy / papa
син	[syn]	son
дочка	[dočká]	daughter
брат	[brat]	brother
сестра	[sestrá]	sister
друг	[druh]	friend
чоловік	[čolovík]	man
жінка	[žínka]	woman
хлопець	[khlópetsь]	boy
дівчина	[dívčýna]	girl
дитина	[dytýna]	child

TRANSPORTATION

поїзд	[póyizd]	train
літак	[liták]	airplane
автомобіль	[avtomobíль]	car (automobile)
велосипед	[velosypéd]	bicycle
автобус	[avtóbus]	bus
човен	[čóven]	boat

LOCATION

місто	[místo]	city
дім	[dim]	house
вулиця	[vúlytsya]	street
аеропорт	[aeropórt]	airport
готель	[hotéль]	hotel
ресторан	[restorán]	restaurant
школа	[škóla]	school
університет	[universytét]	university
парк	[park]	park
магазин	[mahazýn]	store / shop
лікарня	[likárnya]	hospital
церква	[tsérkva]	church
країна	[krayína]	country (state)
банк	[bank]	bank
ринок	[rýnok]	market

HOME

стіл	[stil]	table
стілець	[stilétsь]	chair
вікно	[viknó]	window
двері	[dvéri]	door
книжка	[knýžka]	book

CLOTHING

одяг	[ódyah]	clothing
шапка	[šápka]	hat
плаття	[pláttya]	dress
сорочка	[soróčka]	shirt
брюки	[bryúky]	pants
черевик	[čerevýk]	shoe

BODY

тіло	[tílo]	body
голова	[holová]	head
обличчя	[oblýččya]	face
волосся	[volóssya]	hair
око	[óko]	eye
рот	[rot]	mouth
ніс	[nis]	nose
вухо	[vúkho]	ear
рука	[ruká]	hand / arm
нога	[nohá]	foot / leg
серце	[sértse]	heart
кров	[krov]	blood

| кістка | [kístka] | bone |
| борода | [borodá] | beard |

MISCELLANEOUS

| так | [tak] | yes |
| ні | [ni] | no |

FOOD & DRINK

їжа	[yíža]	food
м'ясо	[m'yáso]	meat
хліб	[khlib]	bread
сир	[syr]	cheese
яблуко	[yábluko]	apple
вода	[vodá]	water
пиво	[pývo]	beer
вино	[vynó]	wine
кава	[káva]	coffee
чай	[čai]	tea
молоко	[molokó]	milk
сніданок	[snidánok]	breakfast
обід	[obíd]	lunch
вечеря	[večerya]	dinner

COLORS

колір	[kólir]	color
червоний	[červónyy]	red
синій	[sýniy]	blue
зелений	[zelényy]	green

жовтий	[žóvtyy]	yellow
чорний	[čórnyy]	black
білий	[bílyy]	white

NATURE

море	[móre]	sea
ріка	[riká]	river
озеро	[ózero]	lake
гора	[horá]	mountain
дощ	[došč]	rain
сніг	[snih]	snow
дерево	[dérevo]	tree
квітка	[kvítka]	flower
сонце	[sóntse]	sun
місяць	[mísyatsь]	moon
вітер	[víter]	wind
небо	[nébo]	sky
вогонь	[vohónь]	fire
лід	[lid]	ice

ADJECTIVES

великий	[velýkyy]	big
маленький	[malénьkyy]	small
добрий	[dóbryy]	good
поганий	[pohányy]	bad
гарячий	[haryáčyy]	hot
холодний	[kholódnyy]	cold
дешевий	[dešévyy]	cheap
дорогий	[dorohýy]	expensive

31

| щасливий | [ščaslývyy] | happy |
| смутний | [smútnyy] | sad |

NUMBERS

один	[odýn]	one
два	[dva]	two
три	[try]	three
чотири	[čotýry]	four
п'ять	[p'yatь]	five
шість	[šistь]	six
сім	[sim]	seven
вісім	[vísim]	eight
дев'ять	[dév'yatь]	nine
десять	[désyatь]	ten

TIME

день	[denь]	day
місяць	[mísyatsь]	month
рік	[rik]	year
година	[hodýna]	hour
сьогодні	[sьohódni]	today
завтра	[závtra]	tomorrow
учора	[učóra]	yesterday

DAYS OF THE WEEK

неділя	[nedílya]	Sunday
понеділок	[ponedílok]	Monday
вівторок	[vivtórok]	Tuesday
середа	[seredá]	Wednesday
четвер	[četvér]	Thursday
п'ятниця	[p'yátnytsya]	Friday
субота	[subóta]	Saturday

MONTHS

січень	[síčenь]	January
лютий	[lyútyy]	February
березень	[bérezenь]	March
квітень	[kvítenь]	April
травень	[trávenь]	May
червень	[čérvenь]	June
липень	[lýpenь]	July
серпень	[sérpenь]	August
вересень	[véresenь]	September
жовтень	[žóvtenь]	October
листопад	[lystopád]	November
грудень	[hrúdenь]	December

PROPER NAMES

Україна	[ukrayína]	Ukraine
Київ	[kýyiv]	Kiev
українець	[ukrajínetsь]	Ukrainian (person)
українська	[ukrajínsьka]	Ukrainian (lang.)

GLOSSARY – ALPHABETICAL ORDER

– А а –

автобус	[avtóbus]	bus
автомобіль	[avtomobílь]	car (automobile)
аеропорт	[aeropórt]	airport

– Б б –

банк	[bank]	bank
батько	[bátьko]	father
березень	[bérezenь]	March
білий	[bílyy]	white
борода	[borodá]	beard
брат	[brat]	brother
брюки	[bryúky]	pants

– В в –

великий	[velýkyy]	big
велосипед	[velosypéd]	bicycle
вересень	[véresenь]	September
вечеря	[večerya]	dinner
вино	[vynó]	wine
вівторок	[vivtórok]	Tuesday
вікно	[viknó]	window
вісім	[vísim]	eight
вітер	[víter]	wind
вогонь	[vohónь]	fire
вода	[vodá]	water

волосся	[volóssya]	hair
вулиця	[vúlytsya]	street
вухо	[vúkho]	ear

– Г г –

гарячий	[haryáčyy]	hot
година	[hodýna]	hour
голова	[holová]	head
гора	[horá]	mountain
готель	[hotélь]	hotel
грудень	[hrúdenь]	December

– Д д –

два	[dva]	two
двері	[dvéri]	door
дев'ять	[dév'yatь]	nine
день	[denь]	day
дерево	[dérevo]	tree
десять	[désyatь]	ten
дешевий	[dešévyy]	cheap
дитина	[dytýna]	child
дівчина	[dívčýna]	girl
дім	[dim]	house
добрий	[dóbryy]	good
дорогий	[dorohýy]	expensive
дочка	[dočká]	daughter
дощ	[došč]	rain
друг	[druh]	friend

– Ж ж –

жінка	[žínka]	woman
жовтень	[žóvtenь]	October
жовтий	[žóvtyy]	yellow

– З з –

завтра	[závtra]	tomorrow
зелений	[zelényy]	green

– Ї ї –

їжа	[yíža]	food

– К к –

кава	[káva]	coffee
квітень	[kvítenь]	April
квітка	[kvítka]	flower
Київ	[kýyiv]	Kiev
кінь	[kinь]	horse
кістка	[kístka]	bone
кішка	[kíška]	cat
книжка	[knýžka]	book
колір	[kólir]	color
корова	[koróva]	cow
країна	[krayína]	country (state)
кров	[krov]	blood

– Л л –

липень	[lýpenь]	July
листопад	[lystopád]	November
лід	[lid]	ice
лікарня	[likárnya]	hospital
літак	[liták]	airplane
лютий	[lyútyy]	February

– М м –

м'ясо	[m'yáso]	meat
магазин	[mahazýn]	store / shop
маленький	[malénьkyy]	small
мама	[máma]	mommy / mama
мати	[máty]	mother
миша	[mýša]	mouse
місто	[místo]	city
місяць	[mísyatsь]	moon
місяць	[mísyatsь]	month
молоко	[molokó]	milk
море	[móre]	sea

– Н н –

небо	[nébo]	sky
неділя	[nedílya]	Sunday
ні	[ni]	no
ніс	[nis]	nose
нога	[nohá]	foot / leg

– O o –

обід	[obíd]	lunch
обличчя	[oblýččya]	face
один	[odýn]	one
одяг	[ódyah]	clothing
озеро	[ózero]	lake
око	[óko]	eye
особа	[osóba]	person

– П п –

п'ятниця	[p'yátnytsya]	Friday
п'ять	[p'yatь]	five
парк	[park]	park
пиво	[pývo]	beer
плаття	[pláttya]	dress
поганий	[pohányy]	bad
поїзд	[póyizd]	train
понеділок	[ponedílok]	Monday
птах	[ptakh]	bird

– Р р –

ресторан	[restorán]	restaurant
риба	[rýba]	fish
ринок	[rýnok]	market
рік	[rik]	year
ріка	[riká]	river
рот	[rot]	mouth
рука	[ruká]	hand / arm

– C c –

свиня	[svynýá]	pig
середа	[seredá]	Wednesday
серпень	[sérpenь]	August
серце	[sértse]	heart
сестра	[sestrá]	sister
син	[syn]	son
синій	[sýniy]	blue
сир	[syr]	cheese
сім	[sim]	seven
січень	[síčenь]	January
смутний	[smútnyy]	sad
сніг	[snih]	snow
сніданок	[snidánok]	breakfast
собака	[sobáka]	dog
сонце	[sóntse]	sun
сорочка	[soróčka]	shirt
стіл	[stil]	table
стілець	[stilétsь]	chair
субота	[subóta]	Saturday
сьогодні	[sьohódni]	today

– T т –

так	[tak]	yes
тато	[táto]	daddy / papa
тварина	[tvarýna]	animal
тіло	[tílo]	body
травень	[trávenь]	May
три	[try]	three

– У у –

Україна	[ukrayína]	Ukraine
українець	[ukrajínetsь]	Ukrainian (person)
українська	[ukrajínsьka]	Ukrainian (lang.)
університет	[universytét]	university
учора	[učóra]	yesterday

– Х х –

хліб	[khlib]	bread
хлопець	[khlópetsь]	boy
холодний	[kholódnyy]	cold

– Ц ц –

церква	[tsérkva]	church

– Ч ч –

чай	[čai]	tea
червень	[čérvenь]	June
червоний	[červónyy]	red
черевик	[čerevýk]	shoe
четвер	[četvér]	Thursday
човен	[čóven]	boat
чоловік	[čolovík]	man
чорний	[čórnyy]	black
чотири	[čotýry]	four

– Ш ш –

шапка	[šápka]	hat
шість	[šistь]	six
школа	[škóla]	school

– Щ щ –

| щасливий | [ščaslývyy] | happy |

– Я я –

| яблуко | [yábluko] | apple |

Other language learning titles available from Wolfedale Press:

Learn to Read Arabic in 5 Days
Learn to Read Armenian in 5 Days
Learn to Read Bulgarian in 5 Days
Learn to Read Georgian in 5 Days
Learn to Read Greek in 5 Days
Learn to Read Modern Hebrew in 5 Days
Learn to Read Persian (Farsi) in 5 Days
Learn to Read Russian in 5 Days

Made in the USA
Monee, IL
12 March 2022

92798346R00036